Contents

BEVERAGES 9

    Cranberry Punch 9

    Cranberry Lemonade 9

    Golden Punch 9

    Percolator Punch 10

    Spiced Tea 10

    Spiced Tea 11

    Hot Mulled Wine 11

BREADS 13

    Banana Bread 13

    Banana Nut Bread 13

    Apricot-Date-Nut Bread 14

    Blueberry Zucchini Bread 15

    Delicious White Bread 15

    Pinwheel Biscuits 16

    Funnel Cakes 16

    Mom's Waffles 16

    Poppy Seed Bread 17

    Date Nut Bread 18

    Orange Marmalade Bread 19

    Mincemeat - Apricot Bread 19

CAKES 21

    Hummingbird Cake 21

    Pecan Upside - Down Cake 22

    Great Grandmother's Angel Food Cake 22

    Raisin Cup Cakes 23

    Eggless, Butterless & Milkless Cake 23

    . Strawberry Pecan Cake 24

    Poor Man's Cake 25

    Date Cake 26

- *Poppy Seed Cake* 27
- *Wine Cake* 27
- *Mississippi Mud Cake* 28
- *Cherry Chocolate Cake* 29
- *A Chocolate Lovers Cake* 29
- *Sour Cream Cake* 30
- *Mom's Apple Cake* 30
- *One Egg Cake* 31
- *Banana Nut Cake* 31
- *Pecan Upside-down Cake* 32
- *White Cake With Grandmother's Swiss Nut Cake Filling* 32
- *Olive's Fruit Cake* 33
- *Fruit Cake* 34
- *Maxine's No Bake - Jiffy Fruit Cake* 35

FROSTINGS 36
- *Broiled Coconut Frosting* 36
- *Caramel Fudge Icing* 36
- *Hard Sauce* 36

CANDY 38

- *Divinity* 38
- *Microwave Divinity* 38
- *Seafoam (brown sugar divinity)* 39
- *Pecan Divinity* 40
- *Peanut Brittle* 40
- *Microwave Peanut Brittle* 41
- *Chocolate Fudge* 42
- *Cheese Fudge* 42
- *Cocoa Fudge* 43
- *Marshmallow Fudge* 44
- *No Cook Fudge* 44
- *Penoche (brown sugar fudge)* 44
- *Mints* 45

COOKIES 46

- *Raisin Bars* 46
- *Gumdrop Cookies* 47
- *Ginger Drop Cookies* 47

Molasses Sugar Cookies	48
Grandmother's Sugar Cookies	49
Crisco™ Cookies	49
Peppernuts	50
Chocolate Haystacks	50
Pecan Balls	51
Sugar Cookies 1	51
Sugar Cookies 2	52
Snowflake Christmas Cookies	53
Chocolate Peanut Butter Cookies	53
Chinese Chews	54
Filled Cookies	55

DESSERTS 57

Rhubarb Pineapple Crunch	57
Homemade Ice Cream	57
Heavenly Hash	58
Cherry Dessert	58
Cheese Cake	59
Christmas Pudding	60
Date Pudding	61
Plum Pudding Sauce:	61
English Plum Pudding	62
Mom's Date Pudding	63
Cathedral Window	63
Mincemeat Graham Roll	64
Date Roll	64

MEATS 66

Pineapple Holiday Ham	66
Roasted Turkey	67
Turkey Gravy	68
Oyster Dressing for Turkey	68
Sage Dressing for Turkey	68
Left Over Turkey Hash	69

PIES 70

Butterscotch Pie	70

Pecan Pie 70
Pumpkin Pie 71
Janelle's Pecan Pie 72
Cherry Brandy Pie 72
Coconut Blender Pie (makes its own crust) 73
Sour Cream Raisin Pie 74
Cream Pie Filling for banana, coconut or pineapple fillings 74
Pie Crust (1 double or 2 shells) 75
Meringue Crust 76
Meringue 76
Never Fail Meringue 76

SALADS 78

Christmas Jello™ 78
Heyen Salad 78
Frozen Strawberry Salad 79
Apricot Salad 79
Cranberry/Pineapple Relish 80
12 Hour Salad 80
Cranberry Salad 80
Cranberry Waldorf Salad 81
Frozen Cranberry Salad 82
Cranberry & Chicken Salad 82
Grandma's Cranberry Salad 83
Pretzel Salad 84
Cherry Salad 84
Lime Jello™ Salad 85
Cucumbers 85
Harvard Beets 86
Broccoli Salad 86

SCENTS 87

Simmering Po pourri 87
Pomander Balls 87
Simple Scents 87

SNACKS & DIPS 88

Cereal Snacks 88

Cracker Spread *88*

Shrimp Spread *89*

Porcupine Treats *90*

Swedish Nuts *90*

Cinnamon Nuts *91*

Toasted Pecans *91*

DIPS 92

Avocado Dip *92*

Spinach Dip *92*

Vegetable Dip *93*

Baked Reuben Dip *93*

Coconut Fruit Dip *93*

VEGGIES **94**

Candied Yams *94*

Broccoli Casserole *94*

Potatoes With Onions *95*

Scalloped Cabbage *95*

Green Rice *96*

Green Bean Casserole *97*

Corn Delight *97*

Scalloped Corn with Cheese *97*

We hope you enjoy this collection of recipes as much as we enjoy bringing them to you.

Happy Cooking!

BEVERAGES

Cranberry Punch
1 3oz. pkg. cherry flavored gelatin

1c. boiling water

1 6oz. can frozen lemonade or pineapple - orange juice concentrate

3c. cold water

1 qt. cranberry juice cocktail - chilled

1 12oz. (1 pt.) ginger ale - chilled

Dissolve gelatin in boiling water, then stir in lemonade or fruit concentrate, cold water and cranberry juice cocktail. Place in large punch bowl with 2 trays of ice cubes or a molded ice ring. Pour punch over ice and slowly pour in chilled ginger ale. Add thin orange slices spiked with cloves for garnish.

Cranberry Lemonade
1/2 c. lemon juice

2c. cranberry juice cocktail (cold)

1c. sugar 1 6oz.. bottle club soda (cold)

Combine lemon juice, sugar, and cranberry juice cocktail. Chill. When ready to serve add club soda. (Ginger ale may by substituted)

Garnish with slices of lemon.

Golden Punch
3 *x* 3oz. pkg. lemon Jello™

1 16oz. bottle of Real™ lemon

9c. boiling water

2 46oz. cans unsweetened pineapple juice

4c. sugar

2 qts. Ginger ale

Mix Jello™ and water as for Jello™. Add remaining water and sugar. Stir. Add lemon juice and pineapple juice and freeze.

Before using, thaw until slushy (3 to 4 hours) and add ginger ale. Pour over ice or ice rings made from part of the punch mixture (without the ginger ale).

Note: This is a very large recipe and very nice to use for such occasions as Golden Wedding etc. Can be made well in advance of use. Always add ginger ale right before serving.

Percolator Punch
Note: Use old fashioned percolator - <u>not</u> electric.

Place into the percolator basket:

1T. whole cloves

1 1/2t. allspice

3 cinnamon sticks

1/2t. salt

1/2c. brown sugar

Put in the bottom of an 8 c. percolator:

3c. pineapple juice

3c. water

Perk 10 minutes and serve hot.

Spiced Tea
6 qt. water

3c. sugar

4 lemons (juice and rind)

6 oranges (juice and rind)

4t. whole cloves

6 cinnamon sticks

Mix together and pour over 3T. loose tea. Let stand 5 minutes and serve.

Note: If desired, this can be made in advance to serve later:

Mix the lemon juice, orange juice, sugar and spices. Heat and simmer for 5 minutes using only 3 quarts of boiling water. Pour over the rinds of the lemons, oranges, and tea.

Let stand for 5 minutes. Strain each mixture and mix.

When ready to serve, heat the remaining 3 quarts of water to boiling and add to tea mixture.

Spiced Tea

Mix and bring to a rolling boil:

1c. sugar

1t. whole cloves

1t. stick cinnamon crushed

1qt. water

juice of 3 oranges

juice of 3 lemons

1/2c. black tea leaves

Add: 1/2c. black tea leaves and steep for 3 minutes. Strain and add 3 quarts of boiling water.

Makes about 24 - 6oz. servings

Hot Mulled Wine

Combine:

1 pint Lambrusco wine

1 qt. Port wine

2 quarts cider

½ c. brown sugar

Place 1t. whole allspice and 1 ½ t. in a tea ball or tie in cheesecloth. Add to liquid along with 3-4 whole cinnamon sticks. Heat until very hot (but do U boil) for 1 hour before serving.

A crock pot works well for this recipe.

BREADS

Banana Bread
Cream: 2c. sugar and 1c. shortening

Add:

6 mashed bananas

Sift: 2 1/2 c. flour

1t. salt

2t. soda

Blend and divide dough into 2 greased and floured bread pans.

Bake in 350 degree oven.

Banana Nut Bread
Cream together:

½ c. shortening

2c. sugar

Add:

2 eggs

3 mashed bananas

Combine:

3c. flour

1t. soda

Add alternately with flour to banana mixture:

*½ c. sour milk

Add:

2/3c. chopped nuts.

*Buttermilk may be substituted.

Mix well and pour into 2 greased pans. Bake at 325 degrees for 1 hour or until a toothpick inserted into the center comes out clean.

Apricot-Date-Nut Bread

Cream together

1/4 cup butter or margarine--softened

3/4 cup brown sugar--packed

Add to above and beat 10 minutes 'til thick

2 eggs

1 tsp. vanilla

Sift together and add to above.

3/4 cup flour

1/2 tsp. baking powder

1/2 tsp. salt

Add to above and mix

1 8oz. package pitted dates

1 6oz. package dried apricots

2 cups walnuts--halves or pieces

Pour into 3 small loaf pans, or regular loaf pan, and bake in 350 degree oven for 1 hr. (or until toothpick tests clean)

Freezes well

Blueberry Zucchini Bread

3 eggs, room temperature

1 cup oil

2 cups sugar

2 cups zucchini grated

3 tsp. vanilla

3 cups sifted flour

1 tsp. salt

1 tsp. baking soda

3 tsp. cinnamon

Dash of nutmeg

1/2 cups chopped walnuts

1 cup blueberries

Beat eggs, then add oil, sugar, zucchini and vanilla. Mix well. Add dry ingredients and blend well. Add nuts and berries and then mix.

Bake at 325 degrees for 60 to 70 minutes in lightly greased and floured pans. Makes two 9x5 inch loaf pans.

Delicious White Bread

2pkg. dry yeast

2T. sugar

2 3/4 c. warm water

1/3c. c. cooking oil

1/2 c. nonfat dry milk

1T. salt

7 - 7 1/2 c. flour

Sprinkle yeast on warm water. Add dry mild, sugar, salt, oil and 3 cups of flour. Beat till smooth. Add remaining flour to make a soft dough. Cover, let rest 15 minutes. Knead for 10 minutes.

Divide in half-shape into loaf and place in 2 9"x5"x3" pans. Let rise till double - about 1 - 1 1/2 hours. Bake at 400 degrees for 30 to 35 minutes. Remove from pans and cool on racks.

Pinwheel Biscuits

Prepare: One recipe basic biscuit dough. Roll dough to oblong shape about 1/2" thick Spread softened butter over the dough and sprinkle with brown, white or maple sugar and cinnamon. Roll the dough as for a jelly roll and cut in slices about 3/4" thick. Place cut side down on a slightly oiled pan and bake as directed for the biscuits.

Funnel Cakes

2c. flour
1/4 c. salt (optional)
1T. sugar
2 eggs, slightly beaten
1t. baking powder
1 to 1 1/2c. milk
Vegetable oil for deep frying

Combine all the dry ingredients in a bowl and make a well in the center. Into the well, add the eggs, vanilla and 1c. milk. Stir the liquid ingredients and slowly incorporate the flour mixture into it, making a smooth batter. Add more milk if it is too stiff to flow from a funnel with a 1/2 inch opening.

Heat a large cast iron skillet about a 1 1/2 inch of oil. When very hot (but not to the smoking point), pour a 1/2 c. of the batter into a funnel with a 1/2 inch opening, keeping a finger at the tip to stop and control the flow.

Positioned over the skillet, begin by releasing the batter slowly into the oil in a spiral pattern.. Fry for about 2 to 3 minutes on each side and then drain on a cookie sheet lined with paper towels.

These can be kept warm in an oven on the lowest setting. Repeat again, adding more milk to the batter if it becomes too stiff. Dust the finished cakes with powdered sugar and cinnamon (optional).

Mom's Waffles

2 eggs separated - beat the whites until stiff.

Add to the yolks - 1/2 c. cream and 1c. milk.

Put together in a sifter: 1 1/2 c. flour, 3t. baking powder and 1t/ salt.

Add to egg mixture.

Fold in the egg whites last.

Poppy Seed Bread

3c. flour

1 ½ t. salt

2 ½ t. baking powder

Combine above ingredients, then add the following in the order given (Part I – then Part II).

Part I

2 ¼ c. sugar

3 eggs

1 ½ c. milk

1c. plus 2T. oil

Part II

3T. poppy seed

1 ½ t. vanilla

1 ½ t. almond flavoring

1 ½ t. butter flavoring

Beat 2 minutes with electric mixer. Pour batter into greased and floured pans.

Bake in moderate (350 degrees) for 55 to 60 minutes or until done.

Glaze when hot (optional).

Glaze for Poppy Seed Bread:

1c. confectioner's sugar

½ t. butter flavoring

½ t. almond flavoring

½ t. vanilla

1/4c. orange juice

Mix together and spread over hot bread with a pastry brush.

Date Nut Bread

Cream:

4c. sugar

4T. shortening

Add:

4 eggs

Mix and work with the hands:

4t. soda

1 1/2 lb. pitted dates

4c. boiling water

Add to first mixture.

Then add:

6c. flour

1 1/2c. chopped nuts

Bake in bread pan (s) 1 1/2 hours at 200 degrees.

Orange Marmalade Bread

3c. flour

1T. baking powder

½ t. salt

½ c. sugar

1c. chopped nuts

1T. grated orange peel

1c. orange marmalade

2 eggs

1c. orange juice

2T. melted butter

Sift flour, baking powder, salt and sugar. Add nuts and orange peel. Stir well.

In a separate bowl beat jam, eggs, orange juice, and butter.

Add to dry ingredients. Mix until moist.

Put in 2 – 9"x5" well greased pans. Bake at 350 degrees for 1 hour or so, then test.

Cool 10 minutes.

Remove from pans.

Suggestion: Serve with cream cheese and additional marmalade.

Mincemeat - Apricot Bread

9 oz. can condensed mincemeat

¼ c. brandy (or whiskey)

3c. flour

1T. baking powder

1t. salt

1 can apricot pie filling

½ c. dark Karo™ syrup

½ c. milk

¼ c. sugar

¼ c. corn oil

1 egg

Grease and flour 2 - 9"x5" loaf pans.

Soak mincemeat in liquor until soft.

Stir together flour , baking powder and salt.

Beat apricot filling, corn syrup, milk, sugar, corn oil and egg together.

Fold in mincemeat mixture and then beat in flour mixture.

Bake at 350 degrees for 1 hour and then test. Continue baking until done if necessary.

Cool 5 - 15 minutes.

Remove from pans.

CAKES

Hummingbird Cake

3c. flour 1 1/2 t. vanilla

2c. sugar 1 1/2 c. oil

1t. salt 3 eggs

1t. soda 1 1/2 c. crushed pineapple

1t. cinnamon 1 1/2 c. mashed bananas

1c. chopped pecans

Mix dry ingredients.

Mix eggs and oil and stir into dry ingredients.

Add pineapple, vanilla, bananas, and nuts.

Bake in 3 layer pans for 30 minutes in 350 degree oven.

Cool on wire racks and ice.

Icing - Have ingredients at room temperature.

Cream 1/2 c. butter and 1 eight ounce package of cream cheese thoroughly.

Add powdered sugar small amounts at a time, blending well between additions.

Thin to desired spreading consistency with milk.

Spread between layers and on top and sides of cake.

Pecan Upside - Down Cake

1c. pecans chopped

1/2 c. sugar

1/2 c. light Karo™ syrup

1t. cinnamon

2T. butter softened

1/2 c. milk

2c. Bisquick™

1 egg, slightly beaten

1t. vanilla

Combine pecans, corn syrup, and butter in 9" pan. Spread evenly.

Stir remaining ingredients until blended and pour over pecan mixture.

Bake at 350 degrees for 30 minutes.

Loosen edges and invert onto plate.

Serve warm.

Great Grandmother's Angel Food Cake

Whites of 12 eggs

1t. cream of tartar

1 1/2 c. (scant – not quite level) sugar

1/2 t. salt

1c. flour 1t. vanilla

Sift sugar, flour and salt together 3 or 4 times.

Fold in slowly to egg whites which have been beaten until very stiff and to which cream of tartar has been added gradually.

Fold in the vanilla. Bake in slow oven at 325 degrees.

Raisin Cup Cakes
Makes 12 to 14 cup cakes

1c. seedless raisins

1/2 c. milk

1/4 c. butter

1 3/4 c flour

1 beaten egg

3T baking powder

3/4 c. sugar

1t. lemon extract

Cream the butter and sugar. Add the beaten egg. Sift flour, with baking powder and add alternately with milk to creamed mixture. Add raisins and flavoring.

Fill muffin pans 1/2 full.

Bake about 20 minutes in 425 degree oven.

Eggless, Butterless & Milkless Cake
2c. sugar

1t. allspice

1c. lard

2t. cloves

2c. hot water

2t. nutmeg

1t. cinnamon

2c. raisins

Combine above ingredients in saucepan.

Bring to a boil and then let cool.

4c. flour

2t. soda

2t. vanilla

pinch of salt.

1 to 2c. chopped nuts

Combine and then add the raisin mixture.

Bake in 350 degree oven until wooden toothpick inserted in center comes out clean.

Frost.

Frosting

3c. sugar

3T. butter

1 1/2c. cream

Cook together to soft ball stage.

Cool.

Beat until thick and creamy and of spreading consistency.

. Strawberry Pecan Cake

1 18 oz. white cake mix

1/2 c. milk

1 3 oz. pkg. strawberry gelatin

4 eggs

1c. cooking oil

1c. frozen strawberries thawed

1c. chopped pecans and drained

Mix dry cake mix, gelatin, cooking oil, and milk. Beat well.

Add eggs, one at a time, beating well after each.

Add strawberries and pecans.

Bake in 3 greased and floured 9" layer pans at 350 degrees for 25 to 30 minutes.

Cool before frosting.

Cake can be baked in a 9"x13" pan.

After cooling, punch holes with toothpick and make filling somewhat thinner than for layers.

Filling

1/2 c. margarine (or butter)

1/2 c. frozen strawberries undrained

1 lb. confectioners sugar

1/2 c. chopped pecans

Cream margarine and sugar.

Add strawberries and pecans.

Mix well.

Spread between layers and on top and sides of cake.

Poor Man's Cake

2 c. raisins

2c. sugar

1c. lard

2c. hot water

2t. cloves

2t. cinnamon

2t. nutmeg

1t. allspice

Put above in a pan and let boil a few minutes. Remove and cool.

When cool, add the following:

1 ½ c. flour

2t. soda

1c. chopped nuts

pinch of salt

1t. vanilla

Pour into 2 layer pans that are greased and floured.

Bake in 350 degree oven.

Cool.

Frost with caramel icing.

Date Cake

½ lb. chopped dates

1t. soda

Pour 1 ½ cups boiling water over dates and add soda.

Let cool.

Beat 1 egg well.

Cream with 1T. butter and 1c. sugar.

Add soda and date mixture and 1 ½ c/ flour sifted together with 1T. baking powder.

Add ½ c. nuts.

Bake at 325 degrees to 350 degrees.

Filling:

½ c. chopped dates,

½ c. sugar

½ c. chopped nuts,

¾ c. boiling water.

Cook all together 5 minutes.

Pour over cake.

Top with whipped cream to serve.

Poppy Seed Cake

To make cake, pour 1c. boiling water over 2/3c. poppy seeds and let stand 1 hour.

Drain thoroughly.

Prepare 1 box yellow cake mix as directed on the label, adding poppy seed to finished batter.

Bake in prepared 13"x 9"x 3" pan.

Cool and frost with desired frosting.

Wine Cake

1 pkg. yellow cake mix

1 large pkg. vanilla pudding (instant)

3/4c. oil

4 eggs

3/4c. (up to 1c.) sherry wine

1t. nutmeg

Beat together all ingredients for 5 minutes.

Bake at 350 degrees for 50 to 55 minutes in greased and floured Bundt or angel food pan. Let stand for 20 minutes before turning out.

Cool.

Cover with powdered sugar or frosting.

Mississippi Mud Cake

Combine ingredients and bake 30 minutes at 350 degrees in a 9"x13" pan.

Melt 2 sticks butter or margarine and add:

1c. cocoa

4 eggs

2c. sugar

1 1/2c. flour

1c. coconut

1 1/2c. pecan halves (or chopped pecans)

While still hot, cover with marshmallow creme.

Cover with fudge frosting as follows:

Frosting

1 box powdered sugar

1/3c. cocoa

1/2c. butter or margarine

1/2c. canned milk

1t. vanilla

Cover top with pecans.

Cool and serve.

Cherry Chocolate Cake
1 fudge or chocolate cake mix

2 eggs

1t. almond flavoring

1 can cherry pie filling

Put the cake mix in a bowl.

Mix the eggs by hand and stir into the cake mix.

Add flavoring and pie filling - folding in gently so as not to mash the cherries.

Mix until the mixture is not dry.

Bake in a 9"x13" greased pan at 350 degrees for 30 to 40 minutes - until firm.

Sprinkle with chocolate chips and chopped nuts before baking.

A Chocolate Lovers Cake
1 chocolate cake mix

4 eggs

1/2c. brown sugar (firmly packed)

1/2c. oil

1/2c. water

1 small carton sour cream

1 small package chocolate chips (melted)

Mix together.

Bake in a greased Bundt pan at 350 degrees for about 55 minutes.

Frost with chocolate icing.

Sour Cream Cake

3 eggs beaten

1c. sour dream with 1/2t. soda

1/3c. cocoa in 1/3c. boiling water

Sift together:

1 1/2c. sifted cake flour

1c. sugar

1t. baking powder

1/4t. salt

Add to the first mixture.

Bake in a square pan at 350 degrees.

Mom's Apple Cake

1 1/2c. sugar

1. corn oil

3 eggs

2 1/4c. flour

1 1/2t. soda

1t. nutmeg

3/4c. cinnamon

1t. vanilla

2c. unpeeled chopped apples

1c. chopped nuts (optional)

3/4t. salt

Mix sugar, oil and eggs. Sift dry ingredients and add. Beat well. Add vanilla, apples and nuts. Stir well.

Bake at 350 degrees in a 9"x 12" pan for 45 minutes or until done.

One Egg Cake

2/3c. sugar

1/4c. butter or shortening

1 egg

1 1/2c. flour

1/2c. milk

1/4t. salt

2t. baking powder

1t. vanilla

Mix in usual order.

Bake in a greased and floured pan at 350 to 375 degree oven for 35 minutes.

Banana Nut Cake

Sift together:

1 1/2c. sifted cake flour

1 2/3cc. sugar

1 1/4t. baking powder

1 1/4t. baking powder

1 1/4t. soda

1t. salt

Then add:

2/3c. shortening

1/3c. buttermilk

1 1/4c. mashed bananas (3 large)

Beat 2 minutes and add:

1/3c. buttermilk

2 large eggs beaten

Beat 2 minutes more then fold in 2/3c. chopped nuts.

Bake in 350 degree oven for 30 minutes for layer cake or 45 minutes for sheet cake.

Cool and frost.

Pecan Upside-down Cake

1c. chopped pecans

1/2c. light corn syrup

2T. softened butter or margarine

1/2c. milk

2c. Bisquick™

1/2c. sugar

1 egg beaten lightly

1/2t. cinnamon

1t. vanilla

In a 9" square pan, combine pecans, corn syrup and butter. Spread evenly.

Stir remaining ingredients until blended and pour over pecan mixture.

Bake at 350 degrees 30 minutes.

Loosen edges and invert onto plate.

Serve warm.

White Cake With Grandmother's Swiss Nut Cake Filling
A wonderful addition to any Holiday meal.

Bake your favorite white cake in 3 layers.

Cool, and put this filling between the layers:

Cook 2c. milk and 1c. sugar until scalding.

Make a solution of 1t. cornstarch and 2T. milk.

Pour this over the sweetened hot milk.

Stir constantly until quite thick.

Draw from the fire, let it come off the boil and then beat in the yolks of 3 eggs.

Cook until it thickens but do not let it curdle.

While mixture is cooling, prepare 1c. of English walnuts (saving the unbroken halves for the top of the cake).

Cool a bit and then add broken pieces (chopped a bit if too large).

Spread between the cake layers.

Frost with white frosting and garnish with walnut halves.

Olive's Fruit Cake

1 ½ c. raisins

1 ½ c. lard

3c. sugar

3c. water

½ t. salt

Boil the above ingredients 5 minutes. Let cool.

Combine following ingredients in a very large bowl.

6c. flour

3t. soda

1t. cinnamon

½ t. each cloves & allspice

1 ½ c. walnuts

Add dates, figs, citron, candied fruits etc. as desired.

Add cooled raisin mixture.

Line 2 or more (depending on how much fruit is added to batter) bread pans with brown paper.

Fill 2/3 full with batter.

Add candied cherries, walnut halves etc. on top for decoration.

Bake in slow oven of 275 degrees for at least 1 hour or until toothpick inserted comes out clean.

When cool, cover tightly.

Best if stored for 14 days or more before using.

Good keeper-up to 3 months.

Slice thin to serve with hard sauce.

Fruit Cake
1c. sugar

¾ c. butter

1 egg

1 ½ c. unsweetened applesauce

2t. soda (in applesauce

2 1/3c. flour

1t. cinnamon

1/4t. cloves

½ t. nutmeg

Cream sugar and butter.

Add egg, then applesauce (with soda).

Sift spices and flour.

Add fruit to dry flour mixture .

1c. nuts

1 lb. dates (chopped)

1c. raisins

1 lb. figs 1c. candied fruit (cherries, pineapple, citron etc.)

Bake in brown paper lined bread pans, filling each about 2/3 full.

Bake at 275 degrees for 1 ½ hours or until done.

Set pan of hot water in bottom of oven for moisture.

Serve with hard sauce.

Maxine's No Bake - Jiffy Fruit Cake

1/2c. dates

1 lb. raisins

1 lb. candied fruit mix

1 lb. pecans

1 lb. marshmallows

1 lb. vanilla wafers (crushed finely)

1 pkg. candied cherries

1 pkg. candied pineapple

1 small can Carnation milk

Mix fruits and nuts. Heat marshmallows and milk in a large pan on low heat. Stir until smooth.

Add fruit, nuts and crumbs.

Put in brown paper lined pans.

Store in the refrigerator - the longer the better!

Frostings

Broiled Coconut Frosting
1/3c. melted butter

1c. brown sugar

1c. coconut

2T. cream

Mix together. Cover cake and broil 3" from heat until golden brown. A good frosting for white, yellow, or chocolate cake and so easy!

Caramel Fudge Icing
1/3c. butter

1/4 c. milk

1c. brown sugar

2c. powdered sugar

1 1/2 t. vanilla

Stir (over very low heat) butter, brown sugar, and milk. Bring to a boil (completely bubbling surface).

Boil for 2 minutes.

Cool until pan is cool to hand.

Stir in 2c. powdered sugar (one cup at a time).

Add vanilla. Beat until smooth.

If too thick to spread, beat in 1/2 t. milk at a time until you reach the right consistency to spread.

Hard Sauce
Combine and blend together:

1/8 lb. butter

1T. boiling water

1 egg white

1 pkg. powdered sugar (enough to make stiff mixture)

1-2 t. vanilla, rum, or sherry wine

Store in refrigerator.

Keeps well.

Use with fruit cakes etc.

Candy

Divinity

3c. sugar

3/4c. white corn syrup

1c. water

Combine and boil until a solid firm ball is formed.

Pour very slowly over 2 egg whites, beaten very stiff, beating constantly.

Continue beating until creamy and it starts to lose its shine.

Add 1 tsp. Vanilla and 1/cup finely chopped nutmeats (optional).

Drop by the teaspoon on waxed paper or put into buttered pans.

Cut when cool.

Stores well in air-tight container.

Microwave Divinity

2c. sugar 1t. vanilla

1/3c. light corn syrup

1/2c. chopped nuts

2 egg whites

Combine sugar, corn syrup, and 1/2 c. water in 4c. glass measuring cup.

Cook on high power for 3 minutes (stirring once).

Cook additional 6-8 minutes (depending on microwave power), or until the syrup forms a very hard ball (almost cracking) stage.

While mixture is cooking, whip egg whites in a large bowl until very stiff peaks are formed.

When syrup is ready, pour it into the egg whites very slowly - stirring constantly.

Add vanilla and beat until stiff and it loses its shine.

Add nuts if desired.

Drop by teaspoonfuls on waxed paper.

Saves well when stored in tightly closed container.

Seafoam (brown sugar divinity)
Makes about 50 pieces.

1 3/4c. brown sugar 1/2c. hot water

3/4c.sugar 1/2c. light corn syrup

1/4 t. salt

Combine in a heavy 2 qt. Saucepan.

Cook covered until mixture boils rapidly.

Remove lid and cook without stirring until mixture reaches a firm ball stage (260 degrees).

While mixture cooks, beat 2 egg whites in a large bowl until they form firm peaks.

Pour hot syrup over egg whites, beating constantly with mixer on high speed.

Add 1t. vanilla and 1t. pecan flavoring.

Beat until peaks form and candy starts losing its gloss.

Stir in 1/4c. chopped pecans and drop by teaspoonfuls on waxed paper.

Store in airtight container.

Pecan Divinity
2c. sugar

1 7oz. jar marshmallow crème

1c. water

1t. vanilla

1 1/2 c. chopped pecans

Bring sugar and water to hard boil.

Add marshmallow crème, vanilla, and pecans.

Stir until it cools and starts to holds its shape.

Drop teaspoonfuls on waxed paper.

Store in air tight container.

Peanut Brittle
2c. sugar

1/2c. water

1t. butter

1c. light corn syrup

1c. light corn syrup

2t. soda

1t. vanilla

Cook sugar, syrup and water to hard ball stage, add butter, peanuts, cook and stir until golden brown.

Add vanilla and soda and stir quickly.

While still foaming, pour on to a well-buttered cookie sheet and quickly spread out.

Cool.

Break into pieces.

Microwave Peanut Brittle
1 1/2c. sugar

1/2c. light corn syrup

Dash of salt

1/2c. water

1T. butter or margarine

1t. baking soda

1t. vanilla

2c. raw peanuts

Put sugar, syrup, salt, and water in 2 qt. microwave bowl or measuring cup.

Cook on High for 5 minutes.

Stir.

Cook another 4 minutes.

Add peanuts and continue cooking on high until temperature reaches hard crack stage (300 degrees).

This is usually 8 to 10 minutes.

Stir in butter, soda and vanilla and quickly pour onto a very well buttered cookie sheet.

Spread.

Cool and break into pieces.

Chocolate Fudge
2c. sugar

2T. White corn syrup

1c. milk

pinch of salt

4T. cocoa

2 1/2T. butter

1 t. vanilla

2 t. cornstarch

Mix sugar, cornstarch, and cocoa. Add milk, corn syrup, and salt.

Stir until sugar dissolves.

Cook to firm ball stage.

Add butter.

Remove from heat.

Cool.

Add vanilla.

Beat until creamy and pour into oiled pan.

Cut into squares when firm.

Cheese Fudge
(my favorite)

½ lb. (2 sticks) butter

½ lb. Velveeta cheese

Both ingredients must be at room temperature.

Blend until smooth.

Then add:

1/2c. cocoa

2 lbs powdered sugar

1t. vanilla

1c. nuts (optional)

Mix thoroughly and put into buttered pan.

Cut into squares.

This keeps extremely well.

Cocoa Fudge
2/3c. cocoa

1 1/2c. milk

3c. sugar

4 ½ T. butter

1/8t. salt

1t. vanilla

Combine cocoa, sugar, and salt. Add milk. Bring to a boil, stirring frequently.

Cook to soft ball stage.

Remove from heat.

Drop in butter and cool to lukewarm. Add vanilla and beat until mixture thickens.

Pour into buttered pan and cut into squares.

Nuts may be added if desired.

Marshmallow Fudge
3 pkgs. Chocolate chips

1 pt. Marshmallow crème

1 can unsweetened condensed milk

4 1/2c. sugar

¼ lb. Butter or oleo

Put sugar, milk and butter together and boil 10 minutes, stirring constantly.

Pour over chocolate chips and marshmallow crème in large bowl.

Beat and add nuts if desired.

No Cook Fudge
1 stick butter or margarine

2 eggs

1 pkg. chocolate chips (12 oz.)

1 lb. powdered sugar

1 t. vanilla

nuts (optional)

Cream eggs and sugar.

Melt chocolate chips and butter (or margarine) in microwave.

Combine together and then add vanilla and nuts.

Pour in well-buttered dish.

Cut into squares.

Penoche (brown sugar fudge)
2c. brown sugar

2/3c. half & half

2T. butter

1t. vanilla

¼ to 1/3 c. nuts (optional)

Boil sugar and milk, stirring as needed to prevent curdling and scorching.

Cook to soft ball stage.

Remove from fire.

Cool.

Add butter and vanilla. Beat until creamy.

Add nuts and put into oiled pan.

Cut when firm.

Mints
(Great for holidays, weddings, etc.)

1 3oz. Pkg. Cream cheese (room temperature)
1/4t flavoring (your choice)
3c. sifted powdered sugar (or more if needed)
coloring

Mash cheese and then add flavoring and color.

Add sugar - as much as possible - with a fork, kneading in remainder as with pie crust.

Roll into small balls. Roll in granulated sugar. Press into candy molds. Un-mold at once onto wax paper and let dry a bit.

Layer with waxed paper and store in air tight container in the refrigerator.

Cookies

Raisin Bars

Cook 1 cup of raisins in 1 cup of water for 10 minutes. Cool and drain, keeping 1/2 cup liquid for later use.

Add 1/2 tsp. soda to reserved liquid, when cool.

Mix these four together

3/4 cup sugar

1/4 cup margarine

1/4 cup shortening (Crisco™)

1 egg

1 1/2 cups flour

1/2 tsp. salt

3/4 tsp. nutmeg

3/4 cup chopped walnuts (addition is optional)

Add alternately with raisin liquid and raisins to the above mixture.

Pour into 13 x 9 lightly-greased and floured pan.

Bake in 350 degree oven for 30 minutes. (May be less - check with toothpick)

COOL WELL and then frost with the following mixture.

1/2 tsp. vanilla

3 Tbsp. margarine

1 cup powdered sugar

2 Tbsp. lemon juice (bottled okay)

Gumdrop Cookies
Makes about 6 doz. cookies.

1 cup soft shortening

2 cups brown sugar (packed)

2 eggs

1/2 cup sour cream

3 1/2 cups sifted flour

1 tsp. soda

1 tsp. salt

3 or 4 cups cut-up gumdrops (**not** spicedrops)

Mix shortening, brown sugar and eggs. Stir in sour cream.

Sift dry ingredients together.

Stir in.

Mix in gumdrops.

Chill at least 1 hr.

Heat oven to 400 degrees.

Drop rounded tsps. about 2 inches apart on lightly greased baking sheet.

Bake 8 to 10 min., or until set.

Ginger Drop Cookies
Makes about three dozen large cookies.

1/2 c. shortening or margarine

1/2 c. sour milk

1/2 c. brown sugar

3c. flour

1 egg

1t. ginger (scant – not quite level)

1c. dark syrup

1/4 t. salt

2t. soda

Cream shortening and sugar.

For sour milk, use sweet milk and 1t. vinegar.

Add egg, milk and syrup.

Sift flour, ginger, salt and soda together, then add to mixture and blend.

Drop by teaspoonfuls about 2 inches apart onto greased cookie sheet.

Bake 10 to 12 minutes at 375 degrees.

Molasses Sugar Cookies

2c. molasses

2c. lard (softened)

2c. sugar

1 1/2 c. hot water

2t. cinnamon

2t. ginger

4t. soda

1t. baking powder

flour to make a soft dough

Blend together molasses, lard, and sugar until smooth.

Add water, then remaining ingredients.

Roll thin and use cookie cutter.

Space cookies far apart on greased cookie sheet and bake at 350 degrees until only lightly browned on bottom.

Cookies will keep 6 months in a covered container.

Grandmother's Sugar Cookies

1c. butter

1t. baking powder

1c. milk

3 eggs or 8 egg yolks

2c. sugar

1t. nutmeg

enough flour to make a dough soft enough to roll

Mix in usual manner.

Roll thin, place on greased cookie sheet and dust with sugar.

Bake in 350 degree oven until lightly browned.

Crisco™ Cookies

3c. flour

1t. vanilla

1 1/4c. sugar

1t. sugar

1c. Crisco

3 whole eggs

pinch of salt. Sift dry ingredients. Cut in fat.

Add eggs.

Roll out, cut and bake in 350 degree oven until lightly browned.

May sprinkle with sugar before baking.

Note: If desired, they may be rolled into a large roll and wrapped in waxed paper, then cut as refrigerator cookies.

Peppernuts

2c. brown sugar

1c. shortening

2 eggs

3 1/2 c. flour

3t. cinnamon

1t.. Cloves

1t. anise

2t. soda in 2t. hot water

1c. nuts

Mix and roll in 1/2 inch round balls.

Freeze.

Bake at 350 for 10 minutes.

Chocolate Haystacks

8 squares semisweet baking chocolate

1c. butterscotch chips

2c. chow mien noodles

1c. salted peanuts

1c. miniature marshmallows

In a large microwave safe bowl, melt chocolate and butterscotch chips - about 2 minutes on High. Stir once or twice while melting.

Stir in noodles, peanuts, and marshmallows until totally covered with the chocolate.

Drop by tablespoon onto waxed paper.

Refrigerate for at least 1 hour.

Store in airtight container.

Pecan Balls
Makes 8 to 10 dozen.

1c/ soft butter

1/2c. powdered sugar

2t. vanilla 2c. sifted flour

1/4t. salt

2c. finely chopped pecans

Additional powdered sugar for rolling (about3/4c).

Gradually add 1/2c. powdered sugar to the butter, creaming thoroughly.

Add vanilla, then add flour, salt, pecans and blend well.

Chill a bit.

Shape into balls about the size of a large marble. Place on a greased cookie sheet.

Bake at 350 degrees about 15 minutes, or until light brown.

Remove and immediately, but carefully, roll the hot balls in powdered sugar until well coated.

Cool them, then roll again in powdered sugar.

Sugar Cookies 1
Makes about 2 dozen cookies.

3/4c. shortening

2/3c. sugar

2 whole eggs

1 1/2c. flour

1/2t. salt

1t. vanilla

Cream sugar and shortening. Beat in eggs, salt, and vanilla. Add flour last.

Stir until smooth.

Drop with a teaspoon (about 4 inches apart) on greased pans.

Bake in 375 degree oven for 10 minutes.

Sugar Cookies 2
Makes 6-7 dozen.

1 3/4 cups white granulated sugar

3/4 cup butter

2 eggs--beaten

2 tsp. vanilla

4 1/2 cups flour

1 tsp. salt

1 tsp. baking powder

1/2 cup sour cream or milk

1 tsp. soda

Cream sugar and butter. Add eggs and vanilla.

Beat 'til fluffy.

Sift flour, measure, then sift again with salt and baking powder.

Combine sour milk or cream and soda and add alternately with dry ingredients to creamed mixture.

Chill.

Roll out on board, cut into desired shapes and sprinkle with colored sugar or sprinkles.

Bake at 400 degrees for 6-10 minutes.

Snowflake Christmas Cookies
1c. butter

1 3 oz. pkg. cream cheese

1/c. sugar

Cream butter and cheese and add sugar gradually.

1 egg

1t. vanilla

1t. grated orange rind

1/2t. salt

1/4t. cinnamon

2 1/2c. sifted flour

Beat in egg yolk, vanilla, and orange rind.

Add flour with salt and cinnamon.

Bake on un-greased cookie sheet in 350 degree oven for 15 to 18 minutes.

Remove from cookie sheet immediately.

Chocolate Peanut Butter Cookies
1/2c. shortening

1/2c. peanut butter

1 1/4c. sugar

2 eggs

2c. sifted flour

1/2c. cocoa

2t. baking powder

1/2t. salt

1/3c. milk

Cream sugar, peanut butter and shortening.

Add eggs and beat well.

Sift flour, cocoa, baking powder and salt and then add alternately with milk.

Drop from a teaspoon on an un-greased cookie sheet.

Bake 8 to 9 minutes in 400 degree oven.

Chinese Chews
3/4 cup flour

1 cup sugar

2 eggs, well beaten

1/2 tsp. baking powder

1/2 tsp. salt

1 cup finely chopped nuts

1 cup finely chopped dates

1 small bottle maraschino cherries, chopped

Beat eggs and add to sugar.

Sift dry ingredients together and mix in date, nuts, and cherries.

Add flour mixture to sugar mixture.

Mix well.

Pour into greased and floured 8x8 inch pan.

Bake approximately 30 minutes at 350 degrees.

Cut while warm and roll in powdered sugar.

Filled Cookies

1c. sugar

1c. shortening

1 egg

1/2c. milk

3 1/2c. flour

2t. cream of tartar

1t. soda

1t. vanilla

Cream sugar and shortening.

Sift dry ingredients together and add alternately with milk.

Add vanilla.

Chill.

Roll thin and cut with round cutter.

Place 1t. of filling on cookie, being careful that it does not spread to the edges.

Place another cookie on top and press down edges with a fork.

Bake 8 to 10 minutes at 400 degrees.

Filling:

1c. chopped raisins

1/2c. sugar

1t. flour

1/2c. water

Cook until thick stirring constantly as it scorches easily.

Cool, and then put on cookies.

Desserts

Rhubarb Pineapple Crunch

4c. diced rhubarb

1 #2 can crushed pineapple

1c. sugar

3t. flour

Arrange rhubarb and flour in a greased baking dish.

Combine sugar and flour and sprinkle over the top.

Topping:

1c. flour

1c. rolled oats

1/2 c. butter

1c. brown sugar

Melt butter.

Add brown sugar, flour, and oats.

Leave crumbly.

Sprinkle over rhubarb mixture and bake 45 minutes at 325 degrees.

Homemade Ice Cream

To 4 eggs beaten well, add 2c. sugar and stir.

Add 2c. heavy cream and beat well.

Add 2t. vanilla.

Place mixture in 1 gallon freezer can and add milk up to the fill line.

Place in ice cream freezer - freezing until hard.

Note: This is <u>not</u> a cooked recipe!

Heavenly Hash
1/2 pint whipping cream

(1c.) 12 marshmallows (or miniatures)

2 bananas

1/2 c. nut meats

1 small can crushed pineapple (drained)

Slice the bananas and add nuts. Cut marshmallows into small pieces and add.

Mix all together with the cream that has been whipped.

Cherries and/or shredded coconut may be added if desired.

Cherry Dessert
1c. milk - heated and to which 40 marshmallows (cut in small pieces- or use miniatures) were added.

Melt and mix until smooth.

Mix:

1 1lb. box finely crushed vanilla wafers

1T softened butter

1/4c. sugar

Divide into half and put one half into an 8"x8" dish.

Whip 1c. whipping cream.

Add 1t. sugar, 1/2t. vanilla and 1/2 t. almond flavoring.

Fold into cooled marshmallow.

Using a tablespoon, spoon half of cream in mixture over the layer of crumbs.

Spoon 1 can of cherry pie filling over the cream mixture.

Then, spoon the remaining cream mixture over the cherry mixture.

Cover with remaining crumbs.

Cover with foil and refrigerate at least 24 hours before serving.

Cheese Cake
Crust:

3c. ground graham crackers

1c. sugar

1T. cinnamon

Filling:

6 oz. cottage cheese

6 oz. cream cheese

2 eggs

1/2c. sugar

1/2t. vanilla

Beat eggs thoroughly. Add sugar, cheese and vanilla.

Beat well.

Pour into spring form pan lined with graham cracker crumb mixture.

Bake 20 minutes at 375 degrees.

Remove and cool for 5 minutes.

Pour the following mixture over the cake:

3/4 pint of sour cream

2T. sugar

1/2t. vanilla

Mix and pour over the cheese cake.

Place in oven for 5 minutes and chill overnight.

Sprinkle with graham cracker crumbs before serving.

Christmas Pudding
2c. dried bread crumbs

1c. sugar

2 eggs

1c. milk

1t. soda dissolved in 1T. water

1c. nuts

1c. raisins

1t. cinnamon

1t. cloves

1t. nutmeg

Mix all of the ingredients thoroughly and steam in a double boiler for 2 hours.

This may be served with sauce or whipped cream.

Date Pudding

1 1/2c. brown sugar

1 1/2c water

Stir until dissolved and put in a "9x13" baking dish or pan.

1c. sugar

1c. milk

1c. flour

1c. chopped dates

1/2c. nuts

1t baking powder

1t. vanilla

dash of salt

Mix and pour into liquid. Do **not** stir.

Bake at 350 degrees for about 40 to 45 minutes.

Plum Pudding Sauce:

Cut pudding slices as desired and steam for 1 hour.

Serve with sauce poured over.

1c sugar

3T. flour

4T. butter

1/8 t. salt

2c. boiling water

1T. vanilla

Mix sugar, flour, and salt.

Add boiling water, stirring constantly.

Boil 5 minutes.

Remove from fire.

Add butter and flavoring.

For lemon sauce, omit vanilla and add 1t. lemon rind (grated) and 2T. lemon juice.

English Plum Pudding
2c. chopped nuts

2c. suet ground

1 lb. dated

1c. currants

2c. raisins

2c. bread crumbs

1c. brown sugar

1t. cinnamon

1t. nutmeg

1/2t ground cloves

4 eggs

1c. warm milk

1/2c. sorghum

1t. soda

Mix all together.

Grease and flour pan.

Steam for about 6 hours in a pan of water on top of the stove or uncovered pan in the oven.

Usually cooked in an angel food cake pan.

Mom's Date Pudding
1c. nuts

2c. sugar

1t. soda

1lb. dates

2 eggs

pinch of salt

2t. butter

2 1/2c. flour

1 1/2c. boiling water.

Pour boiling water over dates, nuts, and soda.

Cool.

Mix sugar, butter, eggs, flour and salt.

Combine mixtures.

Bake 45 minutes in moderate oven.

Serve with whipped cream.

Cathedral Window
A very colorful, rich candy type dessert that keeps quite a long time.

Melt 1 stick butter and 1-12 oz. package of chocolate chips in a double boiler (or microwave on Low setting).

Let cool (not cold) and pour over 1 package of miniature multicolored marshmallows.

Add 1c. chopped nuts.

Pour out onto wax paper covered with flaked coconut.

Shape into long rolls.

Refrigerate or freeze.

Slice as desired.

Mincemeat Graham Roll
16 marshmallows

1 1/2c. mincemeat

24 graham crackers

1t. cinnamon

1/2c. nuts

1/3c. candies cherries – sliced

Add cut up marshmallows to mincemeat.

Let stand 10 minutes.

Add crackers rolled fine, salt, cinnamon, nuts, and sliced cherries.

Form into a roll, wrap in waxed paper and chill overnight.

Cut in slices and serve with hard sauce or whipped cream.

Date Roll
1/2c. corn syrup

1 ½c. granulated sugar

1c. cream

1c. chopped nuts (coarsely chopped)

1 lb. dates (chopped)

1t. butter

1t. vanilla

Cook syrup, cream, and sugar until a firm ball forms in cool water, stirring occasionally to keep from scorching.

Add butter and vanilla.

Stir.

Add nuts and dates and beat until stiff.

Roll in a damp cloth.

Let set over night or until solid enough to slice easily.

Meats

Pineapple Holiday Ham

1 fully cooked ham   (3 to 5lb)

1 can sliced pineapple – saving the juice

1 ½ c. to 2c. brown sugar

whole cloves

Score the top of the ham, using a sharp knife making a ½" to ¾" square grid on top and slightly down the sides of the ham.

Poke 1 whole clove into the corners of each grid.

Place in cooking pan.

Dampen the top of the ham with a small amount of the pineapple juice.

Use your hand to press the brown sugar onto the ham.

Secure the pineapple slices to the top of the ham with wooden toothpicks. Extra slices may be placed in the pan.

Pour the remainder of the pineapple juice into the pan.

Bake in a very slow (275 degree oven) for 1 ½ to 2 hours, basting every 15 minutes with the pineapple juice.

Cool for 10 minutes before slicing.

Remove the pineapple slices and cloves from the ham, disposing of the cloves.

Slice thin and garnish with pineapple slices before serving.

Put ham juice in a small pitcher to serve with the ham.

Adjust the ingredients to the size of the ham.

Roasted Turkey
Select turkey of desired size.

Thaw as directed.

Wash thoroughly, making sure the cavities (neck and body) are clean.

Pat dry with paper towel.

Save the giblets to cook for broth, dressing and gravy.

With your hand, coat the cavities with salt.

Place in roasting pan which has been sprayed with a non-stick coating.

Rub butter or shortening on exterior.

Cover with lid or foil.

Bake in a slow oven - 275 to 325 degrees.

About 1 hour into the roasting, add a small amount of water.

Baste frequently during baking with juice from the turkey.

Baking time will depend on the size of the turkey.

Turkey is done when the legs and thighs pull away from the rest of the turkey.

If necessary, uncover for the last few minutes to finish browning.

Dressing may be put into the cavity about 1 - 1 1/2 hours (again, depending on the size of the turkey) before the turkey is finished roasting.

Cool for 1/2 hour before slicing and serving.

Turkey Gravy
Use the juice from roasted turkey. If additional juice is needed, dilute the juice and use canned chicken broth.

Pour into a saucepan.

Heat to boiling.

Add a thickening made of 1 part cornstarch to 2 parts water **or** one made of 1 part flour to 3 parts water.

Rapidly whisk into boiling broth to keep it from becoming lumpy.

Add salt and pepper to taste.

Cook for 2 minutes.

Oyster Dressing for Turkey
16 cups (4 quart measures) of bread - cube and dry before measuring.

Put in a crock.

Pour enough boiling water over the bread to moisten.

Cover and let stand for 15 minutes.

Add 3 well beaten eggs, 1 quart fresh oysters, salt and pepper (to taste).

Stuff the turkey about 1 1/2 hours before done and continue roasting.

Sage Dressing for Turkey
1 - 2 loaves of bread (or more as needed, either regular white or thin sliced), broken into small pieces and dried for several hours. (Do **not** use buns)

Cook together in salted water: (may be done a day in advance and refrigerated

1 to 1 ½ c. celery chopped (a few celery leaves add flavor)

1 medium onion diced.

Wash and cover the giblets with 2c. salted water and cook covered until tender, adding water as needed. This too may be done in advance.

Mix together in a large bowl: The dried bread, 4 to 6 eggs – well beaten - to which has been added the warm broth from the giblets.

Add the celery and onion with juice which has been warmed.

Stir well.

Season with salt and dried rubbed sage to taste (start with 1t.- 2t.).

This needs to be a very soft juicy mixture. If not moist enough (and it usually is not), add broth from the turkey or canned chicken broth.

This may be used as stuffing for the turkey - placing in the cavity about 1 to 1 ½ hours into the baking, or cooked in a greased baking dish (covered) for 45 minutes to 1hr. in a moderate oven.

Left Over Turkey Hash
In a saucepan, place turkey, which has been cut in bite size pieces, leftover dressing and gravy (or broth).

Add broth or water to thin.

Be sure it is quite "soupy".

Cook for 15 minutes on low heat stirring as needed to keep from sticking.

Put in a greased casserole dish and cover with prepared biscuits, either Bisquick™ or refrigerator biscuits.

Bake as for biscuits.

Remove from oven and serve immediately.

Pies

Butterscotch Pie
2c. scalded milk

4T. flour

2 eggs well beaten

1c. brown sugar

3/4 t. vanilla

few grains of salt

Combine sugar, salt and flour.

Add eggs.

Mix thoroughly.

Add milk slowly (while still quite warm), stirring constantly.

Cook over boiling water in a double boiler until thick and smooth (or in microwave on medium, stirring every 30 or so seconds.)

Cool and add vanilla.

Pour into baked pastry shell.

Serve with whipped cream (or topping).

Pecan Pie
3 eggs slightly beaten

1c. Karo™ (or other) corn syrup

1c. sugar

2T. melted butter or margarine.

1t/vanilla

Stir together until well blended.

Add: 1 1/2c. pecans

Pour into unbaked pastry shell.

Bake in 350 degree oven 50 to 55 minutes or until knife inserted halfway between center and edge comes out clean.

Cool.

Pumpkin Pie

2 eggs

2/3 to 1 cup sugar

1c. pumpkin

1c. scalded milk

1t. cinnamon

1/4t. salt

1t. nutmeg

1/4t. allspice

Beat eggs slightly.

Mix spices and salt with sugar and add to eggs.

Add pumpkin and mix.

Add hot milk very slowly while stirring lightly.

Pour into unbaked pie shell and bake – starting at 450 degrees.

Decrease heat to 375 degrees when crust begins to brown.

Bake about 45 minutes.

Test with knife or shake lightly to determine if pie is done.

Janelle's Pecan Pie
4 eggs, slightly beaten

1/2c. light Karo™ syrup

1/2c. dark Karo™ syrup

1c. sugar

2t. cream

1c. pecans, coarsely chopped

1/2t. salt

Mix together all ingredients.

Bake at 350 to 350 in a 9" deep dish pie pan.

Cherry Brandy Pie
1 ½ c. finely crushed chocolate wafers (approximately 30)

6 T. melted butter

Combine crushed wafers and butter.

Press mixture on to bottom and sides of 9" pie plate.

1 7oz marshmallow cream

1/3c. cherry brandy

1T. maraschino cherry juice

2T chopped maraschino cherries

6 whole maraschino cherries

2 ½ c. whipping cream

Combine marshmallow crème and brandy, then beat smooth with beater.

Fold in chopped cherries.

Beat 2c. of whipping cream to form soft peaks.

Fold in marshmallow mixture.

Turn into crust.

Whip remaining ½ c. cream and cherry juice.

Using pastry tube and tip, pipe on top of pie.

Garnish with whole cherries.

Freeze overnight.

Serve directly from the freezer in unbaked 9"deep dish pie shell.

Coconut Blender Pie (makes its own crust)
4 eggs

2c. milk

1/2c. coconut

2/3c. sugar

1/2c. flour

dash of salt

1t. coconut flavoring

1t. butter flavoring

1t. vanilla

4T. butter or margarine

Put in blender and mix.

Pour into greased and floured glass pie pan.

Bake at 350 degrees for 1 hour.

Sour Cream Raisin Pie

3 egg yolks and white of 1 egg beaten (save other 2 egg whites for meringue)

1c. sugar

1c. sour cream (not commercial)

1/2c. chopped raisins

1/2t. cloves

1/2t. cinnamon

1T. flour

Mix all ingredients.

Cook until thickened.

Pour into baked crust.

Make a meringue with the 2 egg whites, cover pie with meringue and bake at 350 degrees until brown, usually about 10 minutes.

Cream Pie Filling for banana, coconut or pineapple fillings

2c. milk (scalded)

2T. butter

3/4 c. sugar

1/3c. flour

1/8t. salt

2 eggs – well beaten

Combine butter, sugar, salt, flour, and eggs, mixing well.

Add milk slowly, stirring constantly.

Cook until VERY thick and smooth.

Add flavoring.

Cool.

Add fruit.

Pour into shell and cover with meringue.

Seal well.

Bake in 325 Degree oven 20 minutes.

Note: Slightly less sugar may be used if desired.

Note 2: If making pineapple, use a bit more flour.

Pie Crust (1 double or 2 shells)
2c. flour

2/3c. shortening (not oil)

1/8t.. salt

Cut shortening into flour and salt until crumbly.

Add 4 to5 T. cold water to make a soft dough.

Divide dough to fit need.

Roll thin on floured surface or between wax paper.

For shell, place dough in pie plate, trim leaving a 1/2" excess.

Prick sides and bottom of shell.

Crimp and bake at 400 to 424 degrees (depends on your oven), 12 to 15 minutes or until golden brown.

Note: For 2 crust pie, do not prick shell.

Meringue Crust
4 egg whites

1c. sugar

1/4t. cream of tartar

Beat egg whites and cream of tartar until they peak.

Then, add sugar gradually.

Spread in well-greased 9" pie plate.

Bake at 275 degrees for the first 20 minutes, then increase heat until done (time varies, depending on your oven).

Meringue
2 (or 3) egg whites depending on size of pie plate to be used.

While beating, add a pinch of salt, 1/4 (to 1/2) cream of tartar and 3 (to 5) T. of sugar.

Beat until VERY stiff and cover cream filling - being careful to seal the edges well.

Bake at 350 degrees for 10 minutes.

Never Fail Meringue
1T. cornstarch

2T. cold water

½c boiling water

6T. sugar

1t. vanilla

pinch of salt

Blend cornstarch and cold water in saucepan.

Add boiling water and cook stirring until clear and thickened.

Let stand until completely cold.

With electric beater beat egg whites until foamy. Gradually add sugar and beat until stiff (but not dry).

On low speed, add salt and vanilla.

Gradually beat in cold cornstarch mixture.

Turn mixer to high and beat well.

Spread meringue over cooled pie filling, sealing well.

Bake at 350 degrees for 10 minutes.

Salads

Christmas Jello™
Cook 1 package cranberries and ¾ c. sugar in 2c. water with 2 peeled chopped apples.

Cook until tender.

Stir in 1 6 oz. package of raspberry Jello™ and 2c. water.

Refrigerate. Good!

Heyen Salad

1 pkg. lemon Jello™
1 cup whipping cream
1/2 cup sugar
Small can crushed pineapple--drained
1 cup grated mild cheddar cheese.

Make Jello™ as directed on box.

When thickened somewhat, whip.

Whip the cream and add sugar.

Combine whipped Jello™ and cream.

Add drained pineapple and cheese.

Stir.

Put in refrigerator and let set.

Frozen Strawberry Salad

1 qt. (or 10 0z. pkg.) frozen strawberries

1 small (15 oz.) can crushed pineapple

3 bananas

3/4 c. sugar

1 8 0z. pkg. cream cheese (room temperature)

1 8 oz. pkg. whipped topping

Whip sugar and cream cheese.

Blend in bananas, strawberries and pineapple (including juice).

Blend in whipped topping last.

Using paper baking cups, fill muffin tins (24) to make individual servings.

Can also be poured in 9"x13" pan.

Freeze overnight.

Apricot Salad

1 can Wilderness™ apricot pie filling

1 can mandarin oranges

1 small can crushed pineapple

1 c. marshmallows

1c. coconut 8 maraschino cherries

sliced bananas

Mix together.

When ready to serve, add sliced bananas.

Cranberry/Pineapple Relish

Grind 1 lb. raw cranberries and 1 lemon.

Add 1 can crushed pineapple.

Blend.

Let stand overnight.

Add 2c. sugar before serving.

Serve with turkey or chicken dishes.

12 Hour Salad

½ jar pimento cheese spread (room temperature)

½ c. salad dressing

1 c. whipped topping

1 can pineapple tidbits, drained

1 can (2c.) drained fruit cocktail

1c. miniature marshmallow

Mix cheese, salad dressing, and whipped topping.

Add the rest of the ingredients and mix together.

Chill overnight before serving.

Cranberry Salad

2c. water

1 lb. cranberries

1 1/2csugar

1 box lemon Jello™

1c. chopped celery

1c. chopped apples

1c. chopped nuts

Pour water over cranberries and cook until tender.

Strain (save juice).

Add sugar and boil 3 minutes.

Dissolve Jello™ in hot juice. There should be 2 1/2c.

Let mixture congeal, then add celery, apples and nuts.

Place in mold or individual molds.

Serve with mayonnaise.

Cranberry Waldorf Salad
Serves 8 to 10

2c. cranberries ½ c. seedless green grapes

2c. miniature marshmallows

½ c. chopped walnuts

¾ c. sugar

¼ t. salt

2c. diced unpeeled apples

1c. whipped cream

Grind cranberries and combine with marshmallows and sugar.

Cover over-night.

Add apples, grapes, walnuts and salt.

Fold in whipped cream.

Chill.

Garnish with clusters of grapes and cranberries if desired.

Frozen Cranberry Salad
1 lb. cranberries ground

1 – 10 oz. pkg. miniature marshmallows

1c. sugar

1 - 20 oz can crushed pineapple drained

1 pint whipping cream

½ c. sugar

½ t. vanilla

Mix together the cranberries, sugar, marshmallows and pineapple.

Let stand several hours or overnight.

Whip the cream and add sugar and vanilla an mix thoroughly.

Freeze.

Remove from freezer 15 to 20 minutes before serving.

Refreezes very well.

Note: One large carton of whipped topping may be used rather than the cream and sugar.

Cranberry & Chicken Salad
A great luncheon salad!

1 pkg. lemon Jello™

1c. hot water

1/2. cold water

1 c. sour cream

2c. cubed chicken (or turkey)

1 can cranberry jelly (either kind)

Dissolve Jello™ in hot water and add cold water.

Beat in sour cream.

Place meat in individual molds and pour mixture over it.

Chill until firm.

Place slices of cranberry jelly on a lettuce leaf.

Un-mold Jello™ on the jelly.

Serve with mayonnaise if desired.

Note: Finely chopped celery and/or nuts may be added to the Jello™ mixture.

Grandma's Cranberry Salad

1 qt. raw cranberries (ground)

1 ½ c. sugar

Add sugar to cranberries and let stand for 15 minutes.

½ c orange juice

2T. grated orange peel

1c. diced apples

2T. gelatin

1c. chopped celery

1c. chopped nuts

Dissolve gelatin in orange juice.

Add to cranberries along with remainder of ingredients.

Let stand in refrigerator until serving.

Pretzel Salad
Combine 1 ½ c. crushed pretzels, 1/3c. sugar, and 1 stick butter or margarine (melted).

Bake in 9"x9" pan (do not press into pan) at 400 degrees for 7 or 8 minutes.

Stir occasionally.

Reserve ¼ c. of above mix for topping.

Beat 8 oz. cream cheese and ½ c. sugar.

Add I – 20 oz. can of well drained crushed pineapple.

Add the crushed pretzels (except those reserved).

Fold in 8 oz. carton of whipped topping.

Top with reserved pretzels sprinkled over the top.

Chill over night before serving.

Cherry Salad
1 can pineapple tidbits, drained

1 can cherry pie filling

4 bananas sliced

1 ½ package miniature marshmallows

¾ c. chopped pecans

1 pint sour cream

Combine first 5 ingredients and then fold in sour cream.

Chill quickly.

Lime Salad

1 pkg. lime

1 can crushed pineapple-drained

1/2 cup pineapple juice

12 large marshmallows

1/2 cup chopped nuts

1 lb. cottage cheese

1/2 cup whipping cream

Make Jello™ as directed except substitute pineapple juice for 1/2 cup water.

Put on stove and boil hard for 1 minute.

Add marshmallows, stirring until dissolved.

When cool, add pineapple, cottage cheese and nuts.

Let stand in refrigerator 10 minutes.

Whip cream and fold into mixture.

Chill.

Cucumbers

2 cukes sliced

1T chopped onion

¼ t. sugar

3 radishes - sliced thin

2T. lemon juice

2T. chopped dill pickle

1 ½ t. chopped parsley

Dash of pepper

1c. sour cream

Combine and let stand at least ½ hour before serving.

Harvard Beets
A good keeper!

1 can sliced beets - drained (save juice).

To the juice drained from the beets add:

¼ c. water mixed with

1T (level) corn starch,

1/4c. sugar, and

¼ c. vinegar.

Bring to a boil, stirring occasionally.

Add beets and cook until thickened and clear.

Store in the refrigerator.

Broccoli Salad

2 bunches broccoli, cut up fine

1c. sunflower seeds

1 lb. bacon , fried and crumbled

½ c. finely chopped onion

Dressing

1c. miracle whip

½ c. sugar

2T. vinegar

Mix ingredients well, and pour over above mixture.

Toss.

Scents

Simmering Po pourri
This makes a very nice gift.

Combine whole cloves, allspice, cinnamon sticks (broken into small pieces) and pieces of dried orange and/or lemon peel.

Put 1 or 2 tablespoons of this mixture in a pan with about 3 cups of water .

Bring to a boil and simmer.

Add more water as needed.

Re-use until fragrance is diminished.

Pomander Balls
Select firm fleshed and thin skinned oranges, lemons or limes.

Stud the fruit with whole cloves using a nail or skewer to start holes.

Add row after row to cover the fruit.

Decorate with lovely bows of lace or satin and display as desired.

Simple Scents
Soak the desired amount of whole cinnamon sticks in cinnamon oil. Dry. Tie the dried sticks together and decorate these dried sticks with dried flowers and pretty lace or satin ribbons.

The fragrance will enhance any room with fragrance of cinnamon for many months.

Snacks & Dips

Cereal Snacks
1 lb. butter (melted)

1/3 c. (scant – not quite level) Worcestershire

¼ c. Lawry's seasoned salt

1 t. garlic salt (or to taste)

Melt butter and add remainder of above ingredients.

Pour over:

1 - 15 oz box wheat Chex™

1 - 12 oz. box corn Chex™

2/3 - 16 oz. box rice Chex™

2/3 - box Cheerios ™

1 - small sack stick (thin) pretzels

1 ½ lbs. mixed nuts

Stir gently.

Bake in 250 degree oven for 1 ½ hours, stirring gently every 10 minutes.

Cool.

Store in air tight container.

Cracker Spread
1 lg. package cream cheese

Chopped green chilis

Chopped pimentos

Sliced stuffed green olives

Ground English walnuts

Soften cheese.

Add remainder of ingredients.

Let set.

Serve with crackers (your choice).

Shrimp Spread
Approx. 2 1/2 cups

1 8-oz. package Cream Cheese, softened

1/2 cup margarine, softened

1/4 cup chili sauce

2 tsp. prepared horseradish

2 4 ½ oz. cans small shrimp, drained, finely chopped

Combine cream cheese and margarine, mixing until well blended.

Add chili sauce and horseradish to cream cheese mixture, mixing until well blended.

Add shrimp.

Mix well.

Chill.

Serve with crackers.

Variation: Substitute ½ pound cleaned shrimp, cooked, and finely cooked for canned shrimp.

Porcupine Treats

60 caramels (Kraft works best)

1 can sweetened condensed milk

2 sticks (1/2c.) butter or margarine

Rice Krispies™

Marshmallows

Melt caramels and butter in milk in a double boiler or microwave.

Dip large marshmallows into hot mix, roll in Rice Krispies™ and put on waxed paper to set.

Note: ½ recipe will do 1 large sack of marshmallows.

Swedish Nuts
Makes about 4 cups.

½ lb. blanched almonds

½ lb. walnut halves

1c. sugar

2 egg whites beaten stiff

½ c. butter or margarine

Salt

Toast almonds and walnuts in 325 degree oven until light brown (about 15 minutes).

Fold sugar and salt into egg whites.

Beat until stiff peaks form.

Fold nuts into meringue.

Melt butter in jelly roll pan.

Spread nut mixture over butter.

Bake at 325 degrees about 30 minutes stirring every 10 minutes or until nuts are coated with a light brown covering and no butter remains in the pan.

Cool.

Cinnamon Nuts
½ c. sugar

½ c. brown sugar

½ c. water ½ tsp. cinnamon

1t. vanilla

2 ½ c. nuts*

Combine sugars, water, and cinnamon in 3 qt. (or larger) microwave bowl.

Microwave 5-8 minutes (time necessary to reach soft ball stage.)

Quickly stir in nuts and vanilla.

Spread on waxed paper.

Let stand until cool.

Separate.

* **Note:** You may use walnuts, pecans, or both.

Toasted Pecans
2 oz. butter

8oz. pecan halves

Melt butter and stir in pecan halves.

Bake 15 to 20 minutes in a 350 degree oven until lightly toasted.

Stir at least once.

Remove pan from oven and sprinkle with 1/2 to 1t. of salt.

Let cool and serve or store in an airtight container.

Dips

Avocado Dip
1 avocado

1 8 oz. cream cheese

1T. lemon juice

1T. worcestershire sauce

1T. lemon juice

Tobasco to taste

dash of Lawry's™ seasoned salt

Mix thoroughly.

Sprinkle with paprika to serve.

Spinach Dip
1c. sour cream

1c. mayonnaise

2 packages frozen chopped spinach, cooked and WELL drained

1 medium onion diced very thin

1 can water chestnuts, sliced wafer thin

1 pkg. Knorr™ vegetable soup mix (dry)

Mix together and let stand over night.

Serve with crackers.

Vegetable Dip

1c. sour cream

1c. mayonnaise

1t. seasoned salt

1t. dill weed

1t. Beau Monde

Blend, cool, and serve with you favorite fresh vegetables.

Baked Reuben Dip

6 oz. dried beef or canned corn beef

4 oz. shredded Swiss cheese

2 8oz. bricks cream cheese

1 pt. sour cream

1 1/2c. mayonnaise

1tsp. garlic powder

1 small can sauerkraut

Combine all together. Warm in a crock pot and serve with crackers or small pieces of rye bread.

Coconut Fruit Dip

1 8 oz. can crushed pineapple - not drained

3/4c. skim milk

1/2c. sour cream

1 pkg. instant coconut pudding mix (3-4 oz.)

fresh pineapple, grapes, strawberries, melon, etc.

Combine first 4 ingredients in blender and blend for 1 minute until smooth.

Store in refrigerator.

Serve with fresh fruit.

Veggies

Candied Yams

2 cans sweet potatoes or yams

2c. firmly packed brown sugar

1/3c. butter

1/2c. cream

1t. salt

Drain yams and place in a large baking dish which has been sprayed with non-stick spray.

Combine the sugar, butter, cream and salt. Bring to a boil and cook 2 minutes.

Pour over the yams.

Bake in a 350 degree oven for 40 minutes.

If you like, remove them from the oven a few minutes before they're done and cover them with marshmallows.

Return to the oven to brown.

Broccoli Casserole
Serves 10-12

2 pkg. frozen chopped broccoli, cooked and drained.

In a bowl combine:

1 can cream of mushroom soup

1c. salad dressing

2 beaten eggs

1T. onion flakes

1c. grated sharp cheese

Mix all ingredients together and put in a buttered 9" x 12" casserole. Top with buttered bread crumbs.

Bake at 350 degrees for 40-45 minutes.

Potatoes With Onions
3 cups mashed potatoes

1 cup sour cream

1+ cup milk

1/4 tsp. garlic

1 1/3 cup French fried onions

1 cup shredded cheddar cheese

Mix potatoes, sour cream, milk and garlic.

Put 1/2 of mixture in a 2 qt. casserole.

Sprinkle with 2/3 cup onions and 1/2 cup cheese.

Put rest of potatoes in casserole. Bake 30 minutes at 350 degrees.

Top with rest of onions and cheese. Bake 5 minutes.

Scalloped Cabbage
1 1/2 lb cabbage

1c. milk

2T. flour

2T. butter

1/2 t. salt

3/4 c. bread or cracker crumbs

Make white sauce of milk.

Butter, flour, salt, and pepper.

Wash the cabbage.

Cut into large pieces and cook in an uncovered pan in boiling salted water (1t. salt to 1 qt.) that covers it well about 5 minutes or until it is tender. Do not over cook!

Drain the cabbage well.

Oil a baking dish and cover the bottom of the dish with 1/3 of the crumbs.

Put in a layer of 1/2 the cabbage, cover with 1/2 the sauce, 1/3 of the crumbs.

Repeat another layer ending with the remainder of the crumbs.

Bake in moderate oven until thoroughly cooked.

If you desire, remove from oven when almost done and sprinkle with bacon bits and/or shredded cheese.

Return to the oven until the cheese is melted. Baking time varies.

Green Rice
1/2c. chopped onion

1/2c. canned water chestnuts (drained and chopped fine)

1 10 oz. pkg. frozen chopped broccoli

1 can cream of chicken soup

3/4c. milk

1 8oz. Cheese Whiz™

1c. instant rice

salt to taste

Sauté onion and water chestnuts in 2T. oil until brown.

Cook broccoli in 1/2c. boiling water for 10 minutes.

Add onion, water chestnuts and remaining ingredients to broccoli and heat to boiling.

Pour into greased casserole and bake at 250 degrees for 20 to 30 minutes.

Green Bean Casserole
2cans French Style Green Beans

1/4c, cheese cubed

1/2x. water

6 slices bacon - fried crisp and crumbled

1 can celery soup

1/2c. slivered almonds

Add water to soup and melt cheese in it.

Add other ingredients.

Bake 40 - 45 minutes in 350 degree oven.

Corn Delight
1 can whole kernel corn

1 can cream style corn

½ c. melted butter or margarine

1c. Velveeta™ cheese (cubed)

1c. small macaroni (partially cooked and drained)

2T. finely chopped onion

Mix all the ingredients together and bake in a greased covered dish at 350 degrees for ½ hour.

Uncover and bake for another ½ hour.

Scalloped Corn with Cheese
1 can cream style corn

2T. flour

2T. sugar

2 eggs (slightly beaten)

¼ lb. diced cheese

2 eggs (slightly beaten)

1 diced green pepper

½ t. salt

2T. melted butter

Mix all ingredients together and bake in a greased casserole for 45 minutes, or until thick.

www.ingramcontent.com/pod-product-compliance
Lightning Source LLC
Chambersburg PA
CBHW081419080526
44589CB00016B/2600